7. Filling Up The Tank

Text by Barbara Cooper

Illustrations by Maggie Raynor

Series consultant: Valerie Watson

Compass Equestrian

© Compass Equestrian Limited 1996
Setting by HRJ
Origination by Dot Gradations
Printed in England by Westway Offset
ISBN 1 900667 06 1
British Library Cataloguing in Publication Data.
A catalogue record for this book is available from the British Library.

Pony power, like horse power, depends on an engine that runs smoothly, but an engine can only run smoothly if it has enough fuel in its tank.

The fuel-tank of a motor-car or a lorry or a tractor has to be filled only now and again, but a pony's tank (his stomach) has to be kept filled with food and water regularly, every day.

If you have read Book 3 of this series, 'Bodywork', you will know that a pony's stomach is small, but his intestines (or 'guts') take up a lot of space.

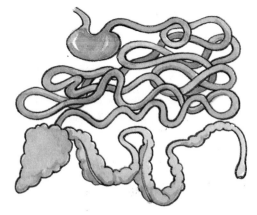

I do **NOT** have a fat stomach – my guts take up lots of space!

Because his stomach is small, he can't eat much food at a time, and because his intestines are curled up like an unwound hosepipe, the food takes a long time to be turned into fuel.

So in order to keep his tank full enough all the time, he spends at least half of the day and night nibbling and sipping.

However, unlike a cat or a dog, who can be left all day with a bowl of food and a bowl of water, a pony's eating and drinking habits need a lot of attention.

In one day, a pony measuring no more than 12 hands (121.8 centimetres) can eat 7.5 kilogrammes (16 pounds 7 oz) of food. That is over 7 times as much as the largest dog and 71 times as much as the largest cat.

A poor, starving pony in the wild, or one who has not been properly cared for by a thoughtless human, would not last three weeks without food. Without water, he would last for less than a week. Unlike a camel, who can live for months without water, a pony needs to drink 20 to 60 litres (4 to 13 gallons) a day.

If the pony is kept out in a field, someone – like a waiter in a restaurant – has to make sure that his meal is satisfactory.

If he is kept indoors, someone – like a room-maid in a hotel – has to pop in several times a day to keep him topped up and mopped up.

Like an elephant, a rhinoceros, a hippopotamus, a rabbit or a hamster, a pony is a herbivore, or muncher, feeding on grasses and certain other plants.

Cats and dogs, like tigers and wolves, are carnivores, or crunchers, feeding on flesh and bones. (The only time that a cat or dog eats grass or another carefully chosen plant is when he is not feeling well.)

Most pony-owners like to keep their ponies 'at grass', which means in a field, all the year round. But because the grass changes as the months go by, you have to check that it is suitable for him.

In spring and early summer, too much rich, juicy grass can make ponies fat, or cause illness. In winter, when the grass stops growing, ponies living in fields need to be given hay, which is dried grass.

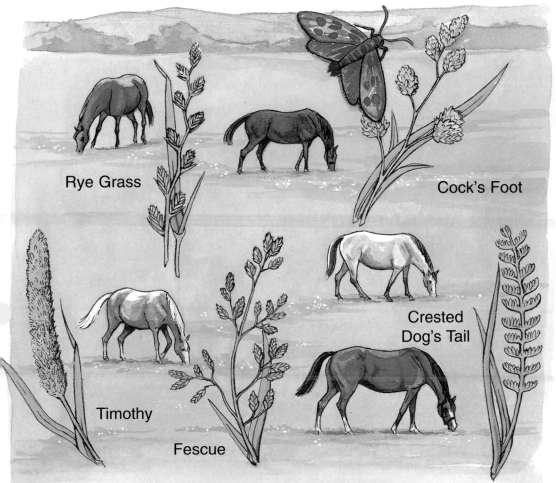

Rye Grass

Cock's Foot

Crested Dog's Tail

Timothy

Fescue

The ponies on this page are all eating the right kinds of grass.

Grass-eating is known as 'grazing', and a pony starts grazing almost from the moment that he sees daylight. Unlike human babies, foals are sometimes born with their milk teeth already in place – so as well as drinking their mother's milk they learn to tear out tufts of grass with their front teeth (incisors) and to grind it with their back teeth (molars).

To reach down to the grass they have to splay out their front legs like a giraffe.

When a pony is grazing, he wanders around with his head down so that he can sniff the grasses and pick out the tastiest ones. He is very fussy about what he eats, and will turn his nose up at grass which is dirty or does not smell nice.

Like humans who drink orange juice because it contains a vitamin called 'C', and who eats bananas, which provide a mineral called 'potassium', ponies sometimes have a need for certain vitamins and minerals. So they will eat fruit such as blackberries and crab apples; chew the bark of certain trees; and even lick soil.

A pony who is hungry, or one who is just greedy, will eat almost anything – including roses, lettuces and cabbages if he can get into a garden. He will even eat plants which can poison and KILL him.

On the next two pages are some of these dangerous and deadly plants.

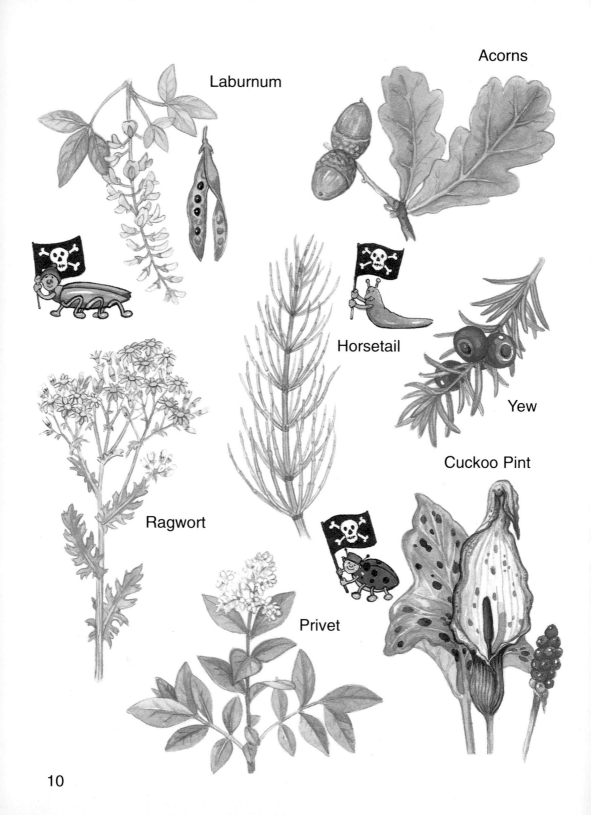

Laburnum

Acorns

Horsetail

Yew

Cuckoo Pint

Ragwort

Privet

10

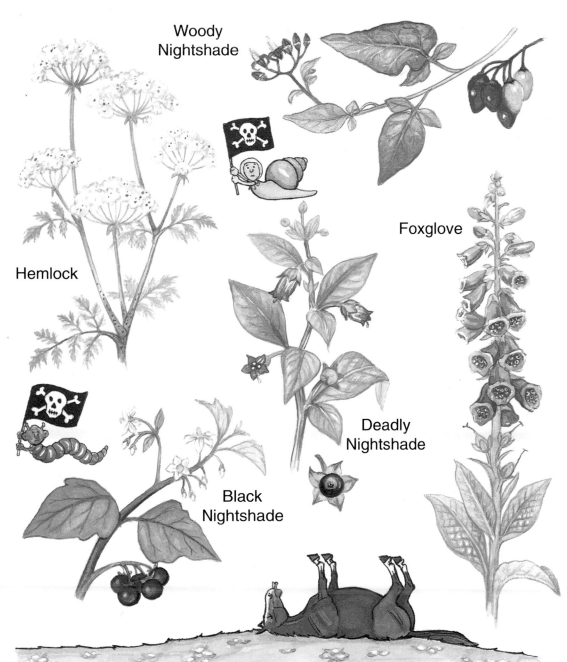

Woody Nightshade

Hemlock

Foxglove

Deadly Nightshade

Black Nightshade

To keep your pony safe from harm you should learn these plants by heart so that you can spot them straight away.

When a pony is kept in a stable, his food has to be different from when he is in a field. And as he was meant to wander about and nibble – not to sit and gobble – he has to be fed little and often. He also likes his meals to be served at the same time every day.

BREAKFAST	7.14
LUNCH	12.21
TEA	4.05
SUPPER	9.46

The type of food will depend on the type of pony and on what he is doing. If a pony is working hard, his engine needs more power, which means more fuel. This comes from 'hard' food. Oats, barley and maize are all 'hard' food.

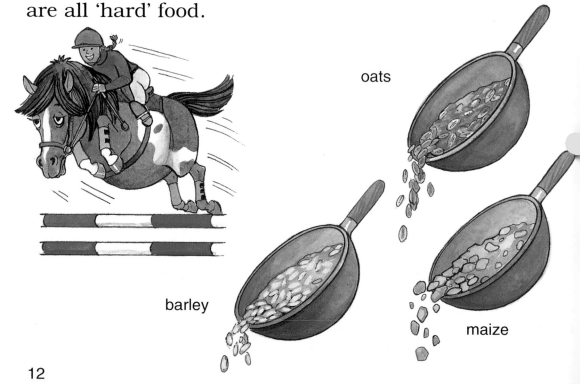

oats

barley

maize

Hard food also comes in 'nut' form, or as coarse mix, some of which is made specially for ponies.

coarse mix

nuts

Another nourishing food is sugar beet, which comes shredded, or as cubes. It must be soaked in water for 24 hours before it is fed to a pony.

sugar beet cubes soaked in water

A 'fizzy' pony, or a pony who is not working hard, will need 'soft' food. Grass, hay and chaff are 'soft' food.

grass

hay

chaff (chopped hay)

To make up for the lack of fresh grass, something should be added daily to the pony's feed, such as apples and carrots. These must be sliced longways, so that they don't stick in the pony's throat.

You can tell if a pony has been correctly fed by
looking at him.

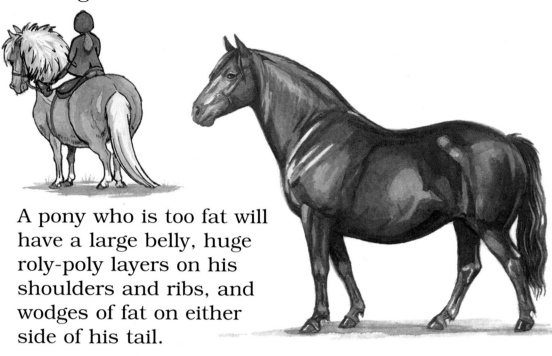

A pony who is too fat will
have a large belly, huge
roly-poly layers on his
shoulders and ribs, and
wodges of fat on either
side of his tail.

A pony who has been given too much hard food may
look well, but he will not behave
well when he is ridden.

A pony who is too thin is a very sad sight. His neck is scraggy. His shoulders and hips are sharp. His coat and eyes are dull and he has no energy.

A pony who is correctly fed will be in tip-top condition – not too fat and not too thin, with bright eyes, an alert look and a shining coat.

The type of feed that you give to your pony will depend on the country in which you live. For example, the basic feed in Australia, New Zealand and the USA is different from that in the British Isles.

Wherever they are in the world, ponies must always have some form of grass to eat. You can learn the reason for this in 'Why Does He Do That?', the next book in this series.

8. WHY DOES HE DO THAT?